I Eat Crow

by Amanda Oaks

Blue Collar at Best

by Zach Fishel

SPLIT BOOK SERIES #1

WORDS DANCE PUBLISHING
WordsDance.com

1st Edition
ISBN-13: 978-0692281598
ISBN-10: 0692281592

Cover & interior design by Amanda Oaks

Author photo of Amanda Oaks by Casey Rearick.
Author photo of Zach Fishel by Johnny Ploch.

Special thanks to Azra Tabassum for
her loving help with the back cover.

Words Dance Publishing
WordsDance.com

I Eat Crow

Amanda Oaks

Blue Collar at Best

Zach Fishel

I Eat Crow

Amanda Oaks

For Kev,
you fucker,
I love you.

Thank you,
thank you,
thank you.

This Always Opens to the Story Within

You've already made it through the thunderstorm
they handed you after you wouldn't buckle
under their burden. You've already pulled
all the hurt from the clouds
so it could wash the dirt off your cheeks.
You jump-started your tongue
after it was muted by the words
swarming above it.
Now, drag your body through the blood trail
of your heartache.
Ride on the rumble of your shame
to the edge of your ease.

It hurts to be so soft sometimes,
doesn't it?

Make the quivering club in your hand
a torch instead of a weapon. That fire
can burn, baby. That rooted light
can bloom bright enough to cause fever
in your knees.

It can be so fuckin' devastating
to realize how red & raw you are
under that dress of slogans
you've been spitting on yourself
since your skin knew stroke.
Since your belly knew flock, hive & herd.

No matter how many times
you turn over a leaf
the shadow is always there.

But there's a window
that you don't have to smash,
lift your flame to find it.
Reach out in time to open it
like summer in your ear
to take in the moment
just before the bird
learns its song.

How To Appear Dangerous

When they come at you with all of your crimes
spilling from their hands to tell you
that you're dangerous, don't shrink.
Believe them. Lift your dress.

Tell them that the city in your soul
never sleeps
no matter how many lullabies
have tried to weave their way
through its streets.

Tell them about the sirens, the glass,
the boys you made messiahs,

the back room at the bar,
the picnic table in the rain,
whose bed you woke up in
the morning of 9/11, don't hold back.

Tell them.

Tell them about the shoplifting,
the slashed tires, the smashed windows.

When they come at you like your skirt
is an invitation, tell them to go home.

When they come at you with fists,
make your face the storm
that will swallow them
whole.

Brush Burn

Sometimes your inner dialogue resembles raindrops
snaking across a car window on a slow afternoon in June.
The treetops disappear into the sky, fog drips from their limbs
& slides down your leg into the gutter of your mind that drives you
to pull off your skin like a cardigan, roll down the window
& chuck it out.

     We swerve.

      You take my hand & we're running through a field
     & the grass is high, it's ripping through our bare legs
    & we're tripping every ten steps & you push me to the ground
   to kiss me. You take my hand & we're dancing wild
to the record player in the dining room of the house
that your mother left you when she died. You take my hand
& a camera & we're filming the way it must feel
to be a bottle of pills always rattling in someone's heart.
You take my hand & we're hell-bent on breaking free.
You take my hand & we're vandals. You take my hand
& we're armed. You take my hand & we're dangerous.
You take my hand & we're lawless & unforgivable.
We felon. We con. We outlaw. We always go too far,
too firm, too fast, slow down, slow down, slow
down, the noose of the land
is still around our necks.

The Tending

Your fingers fumble
through the muddy river
of her hair.

They fish for silver ribbon
to pull out & hang
on the clothesline
that is tied & swinging
in the gentle draft
drifting inside of your ribs.

It drips to the dust
left behind by the boots
that were used
to crush your courage.

That welcome mat
is now a garden
made entirely
of the dry dirt
spilling over
from your lungs:

Two broken hourglasses
wired in & waiting
for the fallout
each time your mouth
is bloodied
by the ground.

I Remember You

I remember you,
your fingers on my back,
caterpillars crawling
across the dirty linoleum floor,
cold air whistling
through aged windows,
the rocking chair on the porch
creaking with each breath
from the sky.
I remember you,
flipping over that rock
& finding a beetle
stuck in the mud on its back,
legs running in place,
so much like a small town bride,
the hem of her dress
gathering water, darkening
her words.
I remember you,
heart made of whiskey,
that water of life
as valuable as gold.
I remember you,
the overturned trucks
in the yard, the rust staining
your cut-off jean shorts
when you would slink
between them
to get to the dirt road
where we would watch
the dust settle
as the cars passed,
twirling wheat stalks
between our fingers
while they hung out of our mouths like tightropes
for anyone but us
to fall off of,

I remember you.

You Flood

It's raining your name & five miles back
my windshield wiper eyes
gave up on clearing the way
you used to mother me into thinking
that it was okay to love me like that.
It's raining your name like the way bones shake
when they are standing in the tallness
& balancing on the hollowed-out surface
of either our love or fear.
It's raining your name like bomb squad,
like battering ram, like fallout shelter.

It's raining your name
& I want it to be hymnal.

I want it to be like two sets of legs
intertwined inside a sleeping bag
in a covered bed of a pickup truck
parked on a forgotten dirt road.
I want it be like the way the body
remembers touch.
The way a smell or a song
can jet ski you back 20 years.

It's raining your name & if it can't be that,
I'd rather it be volcano ash falling over a town
we just mowed over. I'd rather it be
the debris from the crash
between our two airplane hearts
dead-dropping
to the ground.

It's raining your name & I turn slow leak.
I turn puddle. I river. I ocean. I fuckin' tsunami.
You waterboard. You constant drip.

It's raining your name
& I can't seem to remember
the way the inside of my head sounds
without it.

Stranded

A forgotten accordion of folding chairs
parked on a porch carry snow, heavy
on their shoulders.

They hold in breath
the same way you used to
right before I would throw
the last shovel of coal
on the fire between your thighs
just to watch your entire house
go up in flames.

Do you remember
when we found the hive of dead bees
in the backyard of that deserted house?

How we smashed it open with the rust-covered ax?
How we dug out the bees with tiny sticks
so we could cup them in our hands
& blow them off on to one another's legs
just to hear each other scream?

All I ever wanted to do
was eat the weight
off your world.

Devour it all
until I was so fat
with your darkness
that you'd leave me,

that you'd walk away,
luminous
in your own skin.

There is No Shelter in You Anywhere[*]

My wolfpack eyes
watch from the tree line
of your mouth.

Watch waist-high grass
grow out from between
your teeth.

There are too many
bare branches
that lift my dress
then clothesline me
to the ground.

The bears devoured
the door to your throat.

Made room
for the storm clouds
to gather,

made room
for the river
of leaving,

made room
for the waterfall
of stone

but your tongue
is a treadmill of grief
that never stops moving,

a dry, shadowless stretch
where the sun & the wind
eat me alive,

where the cadence
of my feet

striking the ground
are mistaken
for the flaps
of a bird's wings
while we wait
for the rain
to lick
our wounds.

Beauty
is the beast
in you.

*Title taken from Edna St. Vincent Millay's
"I Only Know That Every Hour With You"

How To Remember
After Kristina Haynes

I know a boy that breathes verse into his pillow
& chokes up words in dreams. I know a boy
that only has half a heart because he gave the other half away.
I know a boy that wanted so badly to evangelize me
& all I wanted to do was skew him obscene.
I know a boy that eats handfuls of silence.
I know a boy that cooks everything with rage.
I know a boy whose lips are made of snowflakes.
I know a boy with a tongue so thick with lonely
that they used it to plug the oil spill.
I know a boy that uses trust as a weapon.
I know a boy whose heart is unprotected
by the bowed bars of his ribcage
so girls like us can come & go as we please.
I know a boy that whispers
these breathy fragments of lust at his height
that only can be described
as a full-speed radio dial twist
or the flashing of 300 different
pornographic movies at a swift pace.
I know a boy whose eyes are an ocean of misery.
I know a boy that lets his high-horse
resting outside the door. I know a boy
that wants to run from everything.
I know a boy that coarsened his elbows
on a chipped windowsill
because he would sit for hours, night after night,
hands on cheeks, looking up at the stars
with burgundy-tinted lips & his typewriter
humming behind him. I know a boy
whose throat creaks with the secrets he hides
on the underside of his tongue
because they keep crawling back
on their elbows. I know a boy
that throws apologies around like plates.
I know a boy that you know
& we both know
that he's that good kind of bad news.

How To Forget

You remember how your name
felt in my mouth. How it crawled
into my veins & spun around
in the tide of my blood.
You remember the burn,
the boil, the bite. You remember
the way my heart saved it
from drowning, how it lassoed it
into itself. You remember
how it never really felt honest,
the way we stood, two I's,
two towers of a bridge,
suspension cables pulled tightly—
how the deck between us
was never compromised
by the weight of what we felt
or by the tokens you paid
to cross into me. We were
two I's, two towers of a bridge,
that never could bend long enough
to form the "e" in we— but I,
I remember the war,
when it started on TV,
the pulled shades, the green glow,
Sunday afternoon,
how it was 6,830 miles away
but our empathy knew no bounds,
how all we could do is make love
on the floor, flaming—
to forget.

If Our Beginning & End Shared a One Bedroom Apartment

The day they move in together the End will say,
I know how ugly I must look to you, but baby,
my entire existence is because of you & for so long,
you didn't even know that I was alive, but I,
I watched you. I watched your lips
like train whistles taking off their clothes
so they could collide with everything
that was in front of them, watched you
Desert Storm your way into the thick Middle
fencing us off from one another. I thought
it was because you wanted to touch my face, trace
full moon-shaped patterns around my navel, baby, you
were the most beautiful when you wore your bravery
like an open trench coat running across a packed stadium;

& the Beginning, the Beginning will be terrified,
her stomach will flip over on its back, she'll feel
like a welcome mat in front of the infirmary,
& she'll say nothing. She'll say nothing
because everything she ever believed to be true
already crossed the great divide without her.
The End will try so hard to get her to speak,
will try to kiss the words out of her mouth,
will whisper all the good stories that came
between them into her ears but her lips
will stay pressed together like two books
on a shelf, like two frigid legs.

Every morning, he'll sit her up in bed,
bring her a cup of tea to try & warm
her hands hoping that she'll lift it to her lips
just once. He'll get out the record player
in the afternoons & dance around the bed
like a brush on canvas trying to get her to
bloom into him but there will be nothing,
there will be nothing but winter
behind her eyes.

Every night, he'll settle down into the couch
like a string of red balloons hanging off
the arm of a tree, strung up & deflated,
wavering in the wind & whispering
over & over again, baby, please— please try
to remember how much you loved yourself
before you met me.

How To Swim In the Ocean of Your Bed Sheets

The ocean is spilling out of your mouth
& there's a shark in your chest
that the hull of your body tries to contain
but sometimes, there are no boats
only freight trains parting the water
& they sound like they are rumbling:
Don't hold— don't hold— don't hold your breath.

Ice Storm

The willow tree's plink
when the wind blew
was like passing
an eighteen wheeler
on a road too thin
for two.

The cool calm
of a powerless town
just after, how that
certainty hangs, still
unsure of the sudden
change that transpired
before stunning
everything in view.

The burden before
the first candy apple
crack sets off a chain
reaction that does
a grapevine climb
through your ribcage
to hollow out bones.

It left nothing but
your left thumbprint
carved out & brilliant
on my breastplate—
placed that day
when we only spoke
in old radio purity,
your hook
sitting shiny
on my tongue
before I
swallowed.

We're On Our Own Out Here

Late Summer, picking peas,
cornfield just feet away,
I would tiptoe with the words
of warning looped 'round
every strand of my hair.

When wearing pigtails,
all those locks acting together
could be thunderous
but I would plug my ears & run
in any one direction
until my lungs felt like the tires
of that far-off tractor
I overheard many a time
was plotting my death.

Out there though,
I witnessed the wind
unearth harmony.
The way the stalks
would touch,
sliding against one another
hissing like plastic bags
clothespinned to a wire
& dangling from the mouth
of a paper-winged crow.

I found safety in the squeeze
stuck between clear-cut emotion.
There's something in there
that you can't close your ears to,
like barn rats
or the secrets I found
in the laughter of ghost children
jumping from rock to stone
in the creek bed
behind my house.

Standing still,
before walking in silence

all the way back to the alarm
in my grandmother's voice,
looking up to the clouds
for a way out—
twenty-seven years later
& I still have yet to find it
outside of these words.

Winter Ride 2004

In the passenger seat, I weigh up the past
while the future parks its self like a lemon
on the side of the road white flag shivering
in the wind— riding away from the present,
my grandmother with her dying eyes edged
in red, our hearts spinning like the wheels
that roll us home, both casual
in keeping us alive, but together
having the upper hand
against us
& the northeastern snow.

I said I wouldn't survive
another winter here.

Trees pine for the fervor of the sun,
houses & boarded-up storefronts
go by like boats on a frozen river.
Two-bit hotel taverns
welcoming loggers
& advertising Budweiser
hold secrets dating back decades ago,

snow whipping the windshield,
that I fantasize about smashing
to break free from these classic
guitar riffs padded by grave
silence,

my only way out—
Neruda.

It's just like me
to fall in love
with a dead man.

Eighty-year old words
can do more for me
than the one who grips
the steering wheel.

Nan

How quaint that your eyes rest
over puffed-out pedestals
made just for the weight
of all you've seen.

My fingers skate
through your hair—
complicated like tarnished silver
tangled in the dim light
of the moon.

Age spots— rusted raisins
ironed out like a daydream
you dove into too many times,
draining it of meaning.

Drying your hair, I draw up the memory
of you wrapping me up in a towel
fresh from the dryer.

Cold tile under my tiny feet
as I look out your second story window
to the farmyard shingled with snow.

It's so far from funny
how we've switched places
& I meet you in the middle of my life
eyes-wide-open
at the end of yours.

Time being the only one guilty
of snuffing your candle out
but oh how my fingers will blister
after you leave.

The Lines Will Always Be There
For Nana

Her fingerprints
on the Christmas ornaments
that were once her mother's,
still in the box stamped
1941 Poland,

every single one of them
are hooked & hang heavy
on the walls
of my ventricles
remembering when
we hung them together
four Christmases ago.

Every year since,
I take them out
by their tarnished hooks,
spin them around
to sparkle in the light
from the window
looking for
what she left.

My breath: the chalk
making the lines visible,
almost alive,
underscoring a life
once mixed
with mine.

Sudden Death, Pap's Passing

The phone rang at 3am like an alarm clock
on a Sunday morning in a house
where the family doesn't attend church.

He sat in my belly like a balled fist
as I watched her knees
hit the kitchen floor.

She tells me I used to kick the rib
next to her heart. How badly
I wanted to climb up in there now
& fix what had just been broken.

You were inside me
& I was outside her
& there was nothing
any of us could do

but hold on.

How To Live in the Present

It tells you to meet it where the sky is face-to-face
with the surface of the sea, tells you, *Here, take this*

plate. Sitting on it is a box. You reach out but it's
heavy. Your hand slips. The box hits the water

& opens on impact. You look inside & there is nothing.
You ask for another serving & then another & another,

still nothing. So you climb into the box & you realize
it's your Past & somehow you've locked yourself inside.

Again. There are so many doors but you always pick
the same damn one. You try the knob but it's locked.

You fight with the knob until your hands are cramped
& bleeding. You fight with the door until your shoulders

are throbbing & hard to carry when a note creeps out
from underneath the door. You pick it up & unfold it.

It reads:

*Listen, the last time you were here you broke the door
down so I got a heavier door. I really didn't think you'd*

*be back after that but here you are & when you are here,
you are here alone. None of the others come anymore.*

*You are the only one that relives this memory. You made
this place your home for years. You all did. Each individual*

*inspection process was brutal for me. Yes, I know you
moved out but look, I'm tired, you still show up here*

*every day & I just want to sleep & let's get one thing
straight, once & for all:*

I'm not haunting you. You're haunting me.

34

Don't live with the safety on.

How To Unfold Your Dark

Listen love,
when you're unfolding your dark
it will try to stick its tongue
so far down into your throat
that you'll choke
on all those times
you forgot
to remember,
on all those times
your tone was firebrick red,
when you couldn't forgive
or be forgiven, it's okay
to feel the tears
running down
the inside
of your neck,
it's okay to find
& admire your holy,
it's okay to run down
your mistakes & give them
a kiss, but listen,
when you come across
the first loose string
in your blanket of fear,
yank on that fucker
until there's a pile at your feet,
until there's nothing left
in your mouth to bite off
& spit out,
until there's nothing left
to murder
every single one of your words
before they even hit the back
of your teeth.

Letters of Note

Dear Voice,

You're a sensitive fuck. I get that. It's one of the reasons I love you beyond words. Do you remember how your best friend talked for you in Kindergarten? How they separated the two of you in the First Grade to try & get you to grow on your own? How that teacher made a mockery of you in front of the entire class the first time you let your weird out? Do you remember the girl that hushed you into stillness over your "ugly" saddle shoes in front of the first boy that ever smiled at you? Dear Voice, I'm sorry for not speaking up. I'm sorry for silencing you. Dear Voice, here you are. Dear Voice, take my hand. Dear Voice, the only way to divorce our fear is to marry it first. Dear Voice, I love you. Dear Voice, I vow to continue to love you into the light of your existence.

Dear Sexuality,

I am so sorry. I'm sorry for the label that I seared into your skin. I'm sorry for chaining you to the wall in that dark box of a room. I'm sorry that you were rubbed raw by that too-tight collar. I'm sorry for your empty life, for all those times you nearly broke your neck on hunger when I made a spectacle of you, flaunting your fluidity only for a crowd. I kept feeding you spoonfuls of silence, kept shoving your wild under the dog-eared corners of all those banned books piled to be burned until the clouds turned to one another & kissed up a storm with rain too heavy for any one of us to be dismissed.

Dear Body,

Fuck am I sorry. I'm sorry that during our tour of duty through high school I starved you all day only to go home & binge on a mountain of Bisquick Shake 'n Pour Buttermilk Pancakes while casting tornadoes of Mrs. Butterworth's syrup that would rip stretch mark valleys into our thighs. I'm sorry that I acted like you were invisible the first time I got you stoned just because I had sunglasses on. I thought they were disguise enough to look straight ahead & keep all the words in our mouth. I'm sorry for those two champagne bottle nights just because I couldn't confess my love for the boy that drank them with us. I'm sorry for giving you away so freely. I'm sorry for this mess we're in now but I'm not sorry for you. You mausoleum of madness. You cathedral of chaos. You house made for growing small things. You stood me strong. You stood me when I was the sea & the only thing I wanted was to be swallowed up by myself. You carried me. You languid life raft. When I was trying to burn holes in your sides, when I was all smoke & no fire, two sticks & no spirit you stopped at nothing to save me. Thank you. Thank you. Thank you.

How To Get To the Other Side of the Other Side
After Dick Gallup via Rachel McKibbens

I opened, *You Stupid Bitch* & all I could hear was her laughter.
I opened her laughter & saw she had silver spoons for teeth.
I opened the spoons & found a flood of pills in her mother's mouth.
I opened the pills & found a puzzle of loneliness sitting on a sunporch.
I opened the loneliness & found my grandmother.
I opened my grandmother & found my fears.
I opened my fears & found a well-crafted wall of illusion.

The Train Ride From You

I never thought I'd be here.

The skin on my thighs
vibrating on a train
riding away from you.

Wishing to see bits
of honey-yellow sunlight
flashing through the trees—
instead, it's all overcast
with the Susquehanna
slipping away from my view,
the collapse & swell, you
held that element of danger
like an abandoned baby stroller,
ginger pine needles stuck
in its wheels, you
used to bend my body
into a smooth conch shell,
warm breath softening
my interior overtones
while I hung in the balance
of our harmonics, sermonizing
the structure of our symphony
that I'll now have to learn
how to craft
without you.

My body is trying to push
my soul off the tracks
whispering,

        derail, derail, derail,

while I try to stay steady,
holding on to the notes
that keep me
sound.

Cause & Effect (Saturday Night Bar Fights)

The testosterone
erecting its self
in this space
is sufficient enough
to gag me
way before
my lips
near base.

The stench
of whiskey-dried
lips

that will never
place blows
down on my skin
are prevalent
in all this shit

& the only ejection
I want to be subjected to
is my ass from this seat
& out the door
where the night air
will coat my throat
but won't deem me
its whore.

How To Grow Your Backbone

Take a seam ripper
to the hem
of your silence.

Exhale firestorm—
fever enough
to thaw the blizzard
between the hook
& eye of your bra.

Unchain those tornadoes
you're hoarding in all
of your buttonholes.

Unbraid that cinch
around your waist.

If you're sucking it in,
you can't brace yourself
for the punch.

Bonnet Brave

Small town,
summer evening,

our beer cans
winking
in the fire
fenced in
by our bare legs
parading flip-flops

while the mosquitoes
make a meal
of my ankles,

each brief bite
reminding me
of long-gone
lovers
who nipped
at my petals—
bees
hunting for
short-lived
sweetness
without
promise.

How To Stay Strong
The History of Love Between One Kiss Lock Closure
After *Red Purse*, a painting by Vladimir Kush.

1.
We hung open like a jaw waiting to be threaded to our belly. It was winter. There were not enough workers to fill the third shift so the factory would close down just before midnight. All the underpaid seamstresses filed out to their warm beds & we were left to shiver through the night. I would count the minutes until sunrise just to see your face before you opened your eyes. I would have done just about anything to kiss the cold condensation off your cheeks.

2.
The day she stitched us to our blood-red body she was trying to hold back her tears. Something about finding a paper trail to his infidelity. Credit card receipts, ATM withdrawals, a cell phone bill. She missed a stitch out of sorrow; lined our guts up all crooked. She left her broken-hearted fingerprints inside & out. They lived in all of our corners. Any one that saw said we were doomed from the start.

3.
The first time we kissed we were all arms. Fumbled into each other with too much friction. Time would smooth us over & time was all we had.

4.
We actually believed that nothing would ever come between us. We were all tight embrace beneath the slick wrap of resilience that new love so often brings. Promises were made the night before Thanksgiving but we knew what was coming. We knew.

5.
Black Friday: Their hands were earthquakes. We split open at our fault line for the first time in over a year. Aftershock after aftershock we held on to one another, determined to make it through. Until he chose us. Had us wrapped right at the counter. We left the mall riding under his arm. I looked at you & said, "Here we go, love, here we go."

6.
We waited under the red & green glow of the tree, through their

argument after Christmas Eve dinner, boxed-up & priming our lips for her hands.

7.
The first time she took us out was on a weekend trip. Her cousin was getting married. That little black dress. We sat quivering on her thighs all the way through dinner. We were almost forgotten on a barstool after too many drinks— just to be thrown across the hotel room floor before they fucked on the cheap cotton sheets.

8.
She loved us. She did. But she shoved every godforsaken thing between us. Our body— fat with too many pennies, scrunched up tissues, the too-heavy key set with four keys & six key rings. That horrific perfume that would make you sneeze. The too-tall wallet she would cram into us. Sometimes our arms wouldn't touch for days. The hairbrush: a bed of nails. That time she was all rush & threw in an uncapped pen, blackening our twin souls.

9.
The night she was mugged, the police found us across the street in an alleyway. I will never forget the sound of her heart pounding against us before her attacker snatched & fished around in our insides, the blood charging through his veins rattled with desperation.

10.
When her granddaughter ripped us down one side she was out of breath with fear as she folded us in half & pushed us to the back of dresser drawer. Why she chose to leave us apart I'll never know but that was the first day of our 30 year separation.

11.
The first years were the hardest. I heard you crying night after night & I knew, I knew the rust would have to be brushed from our limbs. I knew our reunion would not be smooth. We sat inches from each other unable to touch. After awhile, there was nothing but silence between us. We had no words left to exchange. We told & retold all of our stories. We prayed for a natural disaster, a clutter-free purge, a new job, a loving set of hands, her death.

12.
Until the day time settled down into us just enough so we were able to reach each other's finger tips. Lightning bolts. Tidal waves. A fuckin' tornado of hope raced through all of our stitch holes.

13.
The day they moved our prison cell to the other side of the room, they never removed the drawers. His back was out for a week. Stupid assholes.

14.
When she died, they all came to help him clean out the house. The air was so thick with sad chaos that we choked on it through our pleas, though our begging that one of them would find heart enough to snap us back together. We hoped that the tear down our trunk would be passed over by all those eyes swamped in grief. We wondered if we would be deemed decent enough to escape the landfill.

15.
Our first kiss back together was full of thorns. We aged apart. Our kind's worst nightmare.

16.
Our thrift store stint was like a second honeymoon. We spent the rest of our days kissing. Prying fingers came & went & came & went—searching for loose change, love notes, tiny treasures that our heart could no longer hold. We swam in that bin full of nothing but each other. Every morning we would admire our imperfections. We would thank each & every one of them aloud for keeping us together. We laughed at the attraction holding together the magnetic locks—oh that young love. We watched how they fought too hard to stay together— how they held on too tightly until they ripped their seams unfixable.

How to Skin a Pisces
For Kurt

I.
I used to watch my grandfather
clean fish at his kitchen table.
One eye, flip— & then the other
would stare down my putty heart.

A pile of heads with hook holes
in their lips, some in their throats,
an omen of what was to come.

II.
I wasn't even fishing
when I caught you,

I gave it up.

My Leo pride
had been watered down
by the fish
that came before you

but you flopped
your beautiful body
all the way up the beach
to the bonfire in my bones
& swallowed my baitless
hook.

I still kiss the tangled line
that dangles
from your mouth.

III.
You have an ocean inside of you
that I could burn on
forever.

Expectant

This morning I whispered,
if the birds were strong enough
they'd hollow out the trees
to make homes.

Under my robe, breasts
hang heavy,

belly slowly swelling
with another name,

little fingers fiddling
with frosty windows
in the next room
while I hug,

knees to chest,
envious

of the steam
making a clean
getaway
from my cup.

For the Birds, May All Beings Be Well

Every year just before Spring,
my skinny legs would wobble a kitchen chair
in the middle of my grandmother's backyard.
The scissor-scissor of the spray bottle
mixing with the sun to border my body
in rainbows.

Comb-comb cut, comb-comb cut.
March's wind carrying with it what fell.

She would tell me the birds needed it
more than I did.

The bendable beauty of my auburn hair
winking in the Spring sun. Weaving in
& out of mud, twigs, bits of newspaper
& string. Whatever she could find
to build a home.

I think of her heart—

four hundred beats per minute,
warming & waiting
for the sharp squawks
that follow,

the constant give & take
that a mother's love
brings.

Ginger

Lining jars of blackberry jelly
next to the green beans,
beads of sweat
strung above our lips,
the clang of boiled jars
over the stove, seeds stuck
between our teeth, berry-
bruised fingernails,
kittens nursing
in a box at our feet,
every summer since I was ten,
a new litter.

His ghost poked the sun today.
I remember how it would dry
our pink bicycle seats. I remember
the way his knees would crack
up & down the stairs. I remember
his rough hands blackened by coal
poking the fire all through every
winter.

Sitting in the strippins,
damp hair snaking & stuck to our backs,
mines beneath our bare legs,
weed torn & etched
with the outlines of flat black rocks
after we peeled them off
like artichoke leaves
never minding the heart
of our matters, remembering
that the dust always settled
in the swimming hole
after we left, just like
his death.

Messages for the Dead

They said you killed him.
Did you?

There's a bicycle tire.
It's sticking out of the heart
of a pond.

It waterwheels
when the wind
snakes through its spokes.

You have dirt in your eyes
& dirt in your hair.
Did you know?

There was hurt
& then a siren,
& the things the newspaper
would never say.

There was a pile of afghans
in a dark room
on top of a chair
sitting in a corner
for years
trapping dust

until we shook it all free.

There's a tree
growing up towards the sun
in a forgotten silo.

Someday
you'll be able to see her crown
from the road.

What the God of My Heart Says to My Heart

The god of my heart says,
I've glittered every doorknob
in your palace of ache.
I've left feathers
on all of the windowsills
to tickle your toes on days
that you can't back down
from your own darkness.

For days
when you can't break your gaze
from the mote of mirrors
that is hemming you
into yourself.

A two-headed horse
trying to run
in two different directions
will eventually
tear itself apart.

But there's a waterfall
made of women
dancing
in white dresses,

there's a river
for you to ride on,

I am not one
but all

of the sharp pebbles
under your knees
when you are praying
for answers.

Since I Can't

When you write us,
write us into the underbelly.

Write me blade
& you skin.

Write us decadent.

Write us into the time
you buried your notebook
at the rest stop
halfway between home
& home.

Write me blood
& you air.

Write us into the pride
of small places.

Write us into the milk
dripping from my breasts.

Write me head,
& you arrow.

Write us into the wound.

Write us into each other
so we can show them

that we will always
make our way out

hand–in–hand.

THE
COLLABORATIVE
SPLIT

Poems BY Amanda Oaks
Zach Fishel

I Remember

After Joe Brainard

by Amanda Oaks

I remember my brother & I hunting for salamanders & crayfish in the creek behind our house, summer afternoons crawled by with us hunched over the water always waiting for the mud clouds to clear after slipped rocks, unstable feet or their instinctual backward darting.

I remember how we lived for Sunday family walks to comb the woods for grape vines to climb & swing from.

I remember meeting at Alaska, the Pavilion, Fire Pond, the Tire Pile, North Camp & the Tannery.

I remember 151 in the church parking lot.

I remember corning cars from Burnside Hill.

I remember trying to navigate Bilger's Rocks on crutches & a cast up to my cooch.

I remember a group of us leaving a party in an abandoned house in the woods to get pizza & returning to find the cops crashing it. That was the first time & only time I was ever in the back of a cop car.

I remember snuff juice rubbed into the school carpets with sneakers.

I remember singing to Reba & Wynonna with my mom, trying to hit all the high notes, I still know all the words.

I remember being 'saved' in my neighbors' garage by their granddaughters who came from Pittsburgh every summer for bible camp in Mahaffey, where Baptismal services were performed in the Susquehanna River in the early 1900's.

I remember Mad Dog 20/20.

I remember when Amber moved here, the only black kid that I ever remember going to our school, her family didn't stay long, for good reason.

I remember 10 cent wing Wednesdays at the Hotel.

I remember helping my mom with wedding cakes & pouring chocolate into molds.

I remember the epic fight we had with the boys after we toilet papered Paul's hunting trailer.

I remember Santa & the Mrs. visiting my Nana's farmhouse every Christmas to give us candy or switches.

I remember stories about Belsnickel.

I remember styrofoam cup boat races in the pond.

I remember lightning bugs in jars with the holes we poked through the top with a churchkey.

I remember a van full of cousins going roller skating on Sundays & while driving home we'd wipe the fog from the windows & search the mountain for the Lady of the Buckhorn in her wedding gown looking for her groom.

I remember gettin' some on the stairs of a gas well.

I remember beers in hands, reckless in the back of a bread truck on some neglected dirt clearing doing donuts & Phil almost backing the lot of us over a cliff.

I remember my arms getting torn up by thorns while picking blackberries all in the name of pie & jam.

I remember being paralyzed in the woods, heart pounding right out of my chest, wondering if the branches snapping underfoot belonged to something I could fight off or if I needed to dash.

I remember Kevin & I riding around in his red Probe. I remember us hanging out with Bill & Fat. I remember him coming out to me. I remember going to prom with him. I remember moving in with him. I remember spooning him after a night terror. I remember always wanting him to outshine the addiction. I remember him & I looking directly at each other laughing so hard we could barely fuckin' breathe.

I remember skinning my knees on the walkway to my Nana's farmhouse.

I remember shucking corn, shelling peas & snapping beans.

I remember my mom breaking her ass sledding with us in the strippins.

I remember Erica & I stopping on a back road at 2am to watch a bear cross through the headlights.

I remember walks to the hatchery to feed the fish with my Pap & the deep feeling of unease that swam in the pit of my stomach after I asked why fish food smelled like fish.

I remember walking out of the Hotel at 2am, every single car in the parking lot had its tires slashed & I wish I could forget what happened after.

I remember a handful of us passing all of L.J. Smith's books between us, my fangirling roots run deep.

I remember Nikki & I writing ABCB poems & printing them out on dot matrix printers.

I remember firehall dances & bingo.

I remember the pool halls in Westover, Barnesboro & Hastings, I rarely played but went for the misbehavior & music, mostly.

I remember moving away a handful of times.

I remember always coming back.

Country Bumpkin Blues

by Amanda Oaks + Zach Fishel

Fat with swallowed quarters, jukebox full of remedy,
a beer-belly of make-a-break-for-it, I need to get-away-
from-it heartache, you see, we feed it until we feel whole.

But the song keeps repeating, each dirty needle dropped
            smack again! (buzzing like a church on bingo night)
As Hank, or Johnny, or some other man with only a first name howls
            out our story.

There is no shallow here, only bottomless pints of a forgiving moon
shining down on the skin of a rooftop too ramshackle
to carry the weight of our holy roller hearts.

The state has smashed its way through the Allegheny,
Susquehanna, Tamaqua, Pine, Spruce, Yellow creeks
in search of oil. Blind to the treasure of tradition,
where pheasant dot the daylight and treestands remain sentinels.

Where doctors are drug dealers with degrees, where cigarette burns
congregate on carpets in trailers that sit on thrones of cinder block
while nodding off in hillbilly heroin hazes, where kids are rarely taught
to trade-in the hand-me-down confederate flags hanging
on their bedroom walls for white ones.

The hum of the bug zapper reflecting the interior of this bar,
where a million gnats sip the edge of plastic cups
awaiting the sting
            (scorned generations of shoeless neglect
playing on the rusted scraps in the backyard)
                        of another hornets nest disturbed.

I Remember

After Joe Brainard
by Zach Fishel

I remember sitting at the Musket, the Alley Popper, Old Corner, Hangar 9, Juniors, the Elks, Moose, Eagles, Pub Club, Italian Sons, Mickey's and some other places that only had two kegs and nothing special except a jukebox full of Hank Williams.

I remember my first time with a girl being on the side of a mountain road, the moon hidden behind Eastern Hemlocks as pick-ups roared towards the paper mill.

I remember collecting cigarette butts out of my pap's yard, each beer can I filled was worth a quarter. He always gave me a dollar and a half.

I remember spit tobacco stains on the porch railings, and squirrels under the feeders.

I remember bluebirds in the garden before the school buses would come and how nastily they defended their homes.

I remember cutting banana peppers bought from an Amish family that was so religious, when one of the daughters told their father no, he put an ink pen through her tongue.

I remember dirt roads and CCR.

I remember a deer jumping through the windshield, the glass in my skin, and a freezer full of free meat.

I remember truck stops and cigarettes on rooftops.

I remember blowjobs on the bus.

I remember moonshine and guitar playing so badly, but dancing in the firelight so well.

I remember Brandon swallowing three plastic bags in the third grade on a dare, his face was an ugly tomato that never ripened.

I remember racing home to do schoolwork as quick as able, grabbing a shotgun and walking the fields, pheasant hunting until it was too dark to find the way back.

I remember sleeping on the porch, my brother talking as the stars hung onto our youth.

I remember the sunset and an arrow, a deer falling seventy yards off in the snow, and the knife opening up the still warm meat that helped us survive the layoff.

I remember the first time I prayed in church, the congregation welling like stoked coal engines, the wooden cross draped in purple robes and a minister telling me to trade everything I am for the truth. I remember not wanting to be anything, and I never prayed again.

I remember the smell of grass and oiled leather from the pitcher's mound.

I remember getting drunk for the first time: fifteen Busch Light and a boxed pizza were all over the yard.

I remember getting beat for not talking enough, for talking too much, and just about everything in between.

I remember buying truckloads of wood stacked in the summer sun, just waiting for the snow to start falling.

I remember bee stings and berry picking, as the smell of elderberries (old boots and lemon juice) filled the house.

I remember grilling everyday of the year out of spite.

I remember the Christmas tree I stole from a u-pick place. We took my dad's money and bought cigarettes, then used fishing line to keep the lopsided limbs upright enough to hide a few presents.

I remember the smells of cow, horse, turkey, pig, and chicken shit. There is a difference.

I remember Myron Cope and chili simmering in the crockpot.

I remember the leaves in October, and how everyone always comes home when the acorns cover the ground.

I remember moonshine until I couldn't walk straight.

I remember the time my neighbor's swimming pool collapsed in a thunderstorm. The boom washed the big girls down the hill, laughing all the way.

I remember hoisting hay bales over my head all day, the straw sticking out of my arms like cowboy cacti I could only dream of for a free dinner.

I remember sleeping in a field of turkey and the smell of snow at the beginning of winter.

I remember getting tattooed after every trip away. Those were some of the only times I laughed freely (But I've never wanted to believe it saved me).

I remember fish guts in the kitchen sink and the time my dad filleted his finger. He stitched it back together with the same fishing line.

I remember kicking my brother from our bedroom window and freezing all night long. He ran away from home and I brought him a sandwich. We got licked for that one.

Blue Collar at Best

Zach Fishel

For the banks of the dirty Susquehanna

On the Porch in the Middle of Nowhere
for Wes McMasters who helped write a portion of this poem

I.

A storm is raging somewhere in Paris.
I've never been there but I've seen you
with a storm raging, in an empty barn
where the bats live upstairs, nesting
like laughter as it watched the coal trucks
race through the back roads where my father
would cut the fences and steal blackberries.
But listen, I'm here and so are you.

II.

I remember imagining what I would become,
what the stars might look like someday.
As a kid my father would point, saying,
"That there is Polaris, the North Star.
It will always guide you home if you're
not here and want to come home."

III.

The constellations are happenstance.
Those stars you see above burnt out long ago
(because light takes time to travel)
and suddenly I've been dead for some time,
dragging my feet right under that star due north
which is probably dead too.

Days are Diamonds

John Prine battles
poison ivy
as chicken chars
on the barbeque
for unwed fathers
clinging to
overtime and
busted knuckles,
knowing we're all
bored children
as the five o'clock news
struggles each day
like a new
toothbrush
in a dirty mouth.

Letter to King Janek (Snowing on a Thursday After Shaving)

Hello brother,

It's midnight and lonesome enough to hear buffalo bones
dancing like Jimi's girls before the fallout,
acid rain in our foothills and foreheads.
Do you remember the psychonauts?
Screaming fire as we grilled burgers
around the ideas of diners and having our own change?
I'm writing to tell you I dreamed of a world full of wires,
frantically pulsing neons and electrophobic folk
dancing like puzzle pieces, all those curves gone straight together.

Ribbons of smoke in your hair was, for awhile, cobwebs swept
out of duct-tape wallets and pennies scrounged
for truck stop travel. We ate pie, had hot coffee with Donna,
the old blond who's been polishing spoons forever.

Keystone Light cracking concrete between the sheets
we tumbled our ghosts in. Rambling at angry sunsets
while smoking on Wesley's roof, or was that before?

Let's meet in Pittsburgh on the North Shore,
catch baseballs from the river to carry back to your kitchen,
full of pierogi and onion, cracked pepper,
and the full longing of a better future.

Skipping Town

Imagine a rotary phone
in a dryer. That's how a heart
operates when driving a hearse.

It never quits on a red light
in the Little Mexico part of a town
where fat kids look up to brothers
with mullets and Lynyrd Skynyrd addictions.

The concrete groans here.

Streets wave as you turn another block
of stolen copper piping
by the bus stop where the sizzled women
painted like clowns grip tatty baggage.

This is how you learn to wake early
or call off work as men parade around
with paper bags of cheap vodka.

That's how a heart gets confused
between the mission shelters and cathedrals.
It requires your whole hand turning just to leave.

Blue Collar at Best

Unraveling
train
wrecked

against
basement hotels
knowing no

thing bounces back
up from where it
dropped.

Eating Alone

There's a certain way to move the left hand
when flipping eggs for a woman whose heart
is still asleep.

You will fail and break the yolks,
watching perfect yellow ribbons
string themselves across the skillet,
hardening at the first bit of heat
like winter traffic.

You are the brown paper towels
used in second grade
to see how much impact
lipstick will one day make.

You're dancing in the ocean,
kelp falling across your breasts,
a mermaid dangling in the moonlight
as the tide rolls in.

This desire is a greasy spoon
found on the counter
after soaking your sleeves all day
for minimum wage.

You reach into the basin,
earn a pinky scar
from some careless hand
throwing cake cutters.

Some minuscule parts per millionth
leave your body, heavy lightning
marrying the filth
as a shark turns southward
against the current.

Your fear
in its ragged mouth.

Horsetails

The cirrus above were horsetails
running from the smoke stacks
as we latched flaps and buckled coats,
holding out for incredible thunderings,
standing long as the mud of the dirty Susquehanna
where girls lose virginity to four wheel drives
and lift kits.

We go on working despite our Sunday ghosts.
Here, mothers use food stamps for cigarettes
and children learn to talk to rabbits or fall asleep
to infomercials.

Parades drum on to resemble community
but the trailer parks know better,
sharing lovers and thirty packs,
having yard sales for angry fixes
while school boys are mauled in saw mills
and two keg bars.

My Nana's Larynx Doesn't Sing, it Hollers

She speaks verse learned in day school
or spends the hours nosing through the paper
exclaiming so-and-so died as if I was around

for the old parties Shirley and Bill would drive a
dirty old Chevy out to, where my father would tease
Uncle Dave for believing in aliens.

"Hell, he'd get all dressed up on a motorbike with
a Polaroid camera and go through the strippins
like he was gonna catch one."

She sneezes in fits during hockey games.
One sniffle erupting into pageantries of snot
lasting whole periods unless we're losing then it's cussing

the team for not scoring, "Even if the goalies were to go on strike.
Those asshole refs." Followed by her asking forgiveness
from a god who took too many grandchildren.

Just praying, and praying about things,
until her teacup dynasty is washed clean with age,
the thirteen barely practiced names scrawled across the bottoms
as she demands of us all, "Yinz quit goofin' off.
There's pop and hoagies in the fridge."

Wanting

An empty coffin

  makes so much noise

compared to what we can handle.

Personal Poem #26
   After Ted Berrigan

       Time has left its mark
like a battered wife. The court costs
are too   much to handle
suitcases while turtles slow down violently.
July makes snowstorms of all this fluff
at the dollar general
where women with bad teeth scream
at ugly children lifting lipstick.
Sister's turning prettier than
dead willows that won't stop swinging
where
        trees can still sing. Appalachia
        is beards and baldness
growing into love until I like
things enough to   continue.
        My ears are forests counting
        the stretch marks of flat moons
        as a tall Jewish woman carries shapes
        in her
                eyes and
lets everyone drink cheap
        until two (on the porch only).
        Hammocks roll over ashtrays.
Pigs play accordion in the wind
, as the dog days get hotter.
It would be easier to work a solid week,
vacation once a year to an ocean
town like Myrtle Beach,
        but who would account for the beauty?
Where would the clouds come sit?
Is there even a question   (there's always some)
left to the boys grown too scared
to do anything but sit
        inside single bedroom
apartments waiting to be drunk again?
Fleas stay desperate, the lonely dig
scabs just to taste some body.

Sisters turning prettier,
        playing desperately in the marching band
at a DUI checkpoint.

I Left and Bloomed

We used to make
plywood ramps
with a cinder block
or an old tire
and see who could
jump the highest
on peddle bikes.
Nobody ever went
into the sky,
but a lot of us
dreamed about it.
Some of us left town,
looking for better
horizons and getting
dirty windows.
Most of us stayed,
starting families
that would never leave,
like our parents
or the weeds.

Going Away

The rain had let up from swallowing Ohio
while he stared at her hipbones
during lecture. She'd stretch and he'd think of
stealing library books like Ted Berrigan,
reading them to her molars in the mornings
while her boyfriend poured
cement on the docks of Lake Erie.
They'd walked along the Maumee once,
watching the mud wash up Sheepshead
and Styrofoam. He asked if she would remember
how the sunset was its own explosion out here.
Here, where everyone's familiar enough to use
the side door, and nostalgia is a quiet lunch of
fried cheese and a burger, alternating on picking
up the tab for several months now.

Summer in Paper Mill Town

The mills
burn pulp

farting into the
atmosphere

clinging
clothing

makes everyone
dress how they feel

cooking chicken
thighs or beef

heart with vegetables
pulled from the garden

as radios
wore out in the sun.

Meanest Dog in Town

The neighbors were strung out
like telephone wires heavy
with dead squirrels, orphaned shoes,
and busted starlight.
Their dog was vicious,
snarling from the rusted
chain meshed into his neck as
he'd guard the children without shoes,
freeze-pops smeared around their sticky lips.
Generic macaroni in paper bowls collected
dirty clouds of flies as the paperboy heaved
yellowed newspapers against the broken steps.
Dog shit piled in the driveway while
the kids went to school for free lunches.
When the truck thumped his skeletal frame
the gravel skidded as intestines came from his ass
and blood leaked like a sad bucket from his ears.
The flies moved from the bowls to his eyes
as they shriveled in the sun,
silently looking onward as the children
played in the street.

Christmas Eve 1998

It was between the weather capital of the world
and my Nana's house just as the ham was pulled
from the oven, pineapple glazing slick as the snow
being kicked over the mountain when

the buggy trudged its way home.
The horse was strong and wet against the traffic lights,
steaming across route 119 northbound with the familiarity
of Orion in the night sky before oak splintered

for a good eighty yards. The ambulances were a bad
string of lights, blinking and heaped along the highway
as the radio faded from carols to the sound of windshield
wipers moving faster than the road.

Trout Fishing in the Past

As the coals died down,
I'd split the flesh of rainbows,
wrapped in silver linings.
Squeezed lemons and
onion julienned against
the wooden tables
where my uncles played cards,
sopping up bacon grease from
breakfast or bourbon
the night before.
The fish would flake,
eyes glazed,
yellowed Yukons
so fickle in the afterglow
of a touch,
sucked from the bones
and forgotten.

Seeing Magritte in a Tiger's House

He was lying in the bedroom,
eyes adjusting to Empire of Light
as the snow worked itself
into the blinds. She stretched her bones
reflecting his venerations
against the window as the clouds
fell into view with the street outside.
He would say, *you are very beautiful,*
first thing each morning— that day
the ashcans were preparing
for another storm as everything
would be in white, again.
Her darkness was a small cache of houses
swallowed in the trees before
disappearing to turn the shower as hot as it could get.
He indulged in her slowness,
thankful to be twenty minutes behind
for the rest of his life, and proud of the way
she sat next to him, sharing food in the cafes
while other couples opposed each other.

3/28/13

It was where I first bagged produce for old women
as their blue-gray hair reflected the bruises
of December sunsets. The woman was always
working late, checking the cameras out back where
kids from trade-school installed spoilers on their
junk cars, leaving black patches in the parking lot on Fridays.
They said she was already dead, stuck in her cellophane
behind the counter, even before the officer had duct-taped
her wrists into mangled cuts of meat drug across driveways
while the neighbors shoveled their snow.
Everyone heard the buckshot bounce through the carts as wads
of creamed corn and Spam scrambled into aimless rage
down the checkout line. The shotgun hung like cord phones,
a heavy silence on the tiles I used to mop every night at ten.

Enough

Sawdust clings to the tired
tires of tractors

treading dawn
so flatly against

the dewed hoods
of rusty trucks

as thermoses
fill their holders

and men with
dirty palms

hold their
wives in an embrace

braver than the up
turned soil

struggling
every season

beginning each
morning

with enough trust
that it will be again.

Secrets in the Front Seat
for Sage Lucas

Well that's how it goes
if it was going anywhere.

If I was going anywhere—
dying I'm not sure what I would say

or what I would
say I've done

except chase windmills
in search of quiet funerals,

which might be the best kind,
but I don't want them to be my kind.

Baseball Season is Boring

Watching old reels of Ali chopping
on Ron Lyle sounds like a butchers' block
of used song titles as outside the trees break
like small breasted women.
The syllogisms are dumber than slicing onions
in your hand. There's blood in the macaroni
salad while outside maples dance until the green
sparks mimic the sleeping bears of summer.
The little things kill us, bent clothes hangars and
how the upper peninsula of the state is rusting
like clipped angels in bad karaoke bars.
Mirrors in abandoned houses where padlocks wait.
Gargoyles crumbling on waterspouts. We're ill equipped
for shattering in left field with mitts too small,
wearing out like cigarette burns in a passenger seat.

Car Crashes and Mustaches

There was mostly dust
and a ringing
inside the Chevy
as I stumbled out
laughing under the
streetlights. Twenty feet
of accident kept me
from sliding the wrong
direction despite
smelling of burning
marijuana, someone's dog
and the impossible
loneliness of coats for most of the
last three years. The front
axles were arms
stretching as the drugs
were sunk in the sound
hole of my favorite
guitar. Everyone loves being
Bob Dylan except Bob Dylan.
Puking in the grass
was easy, fireflies dotting
the fields like pimples
on freshman lit. majors
with their knees
folding over like the
dog-eared pages of
poets. The humming was
just a sucker
punch.

Personal Values

      The scent of sparklers and warm beer played whiffle ball with the neighborhood as hotdogs cooked and elephants swung along the freeway, their trunks rumbling for attention, falling when they thought nobody was around.

On a Friend Dying Inside the House
for Johnny Ploch

In the attic were a myriad of Frisbees from the time
we hucked discs in kite-winds,
terrified of the gale of misguidance,
saxophones in alleys and Kerouac
                going   going   going like
upholstered couches,
each stain sticking
and loosening the stitches.
I miss the juvenile
                    sledding in parking lots,
drifting laughter wagging in the trees.

Pointless as new pencils,
the Daffodils warm on his grave,
        making the most articulate choke for sunlight.

Cardiology (Letter to a Monk in MA)
for Glen Vandermark

Every time I tear a bucket of chicken in half
to fit the weak-mouthed plastic bags of uncommitted trash cans,
I make sure to become a tractor. Smeared bright glossy ketchup,
    my fingers greased pistons pumping crude oil like the

giant earth turners your dad taught you to drink on. Big wheels

keep on turning

dragging

    plaque in the drive-thru of my heart.

Remember drinking whiskey from green glass until
    I punched your sister 's face? I don't,

but I do remember carving an ugly moon right through my father's
tomato patch, a six-pack bungee corded to the back of my mower.
Never again was I allowed to watch the leaves spray from the guard,
chunks of vegetable hewn all over, a real tossed salad dripping with
piss and vinegar.

    I called you in tears, the blade bent, toppled again
    the horseshoe pit came from the zucchini blossoms

your laughter saying

    flowers kill us all dummy,

    Subclavian Arteries
    Brachiocephalic trunk
Aorta made from grizzly bones and something

always about pulmonaries as the sunbeams burned rainbows
in the atrium like the trout you and I used to cook out behind
J. Central Trucking in our secret creek. With great heat on the foil,
I'd have to cut

the heads from the fish

even though they're lucky, because you never could stomach
death, even one this delicious.
    Coal trucks rumbled in the gut old man style

along the hills with beer bottles in our pockets,
harvest moon and a baby coyote in the dirt. You held its
    scruff neck like a shaman, howling with it above
    your head:

Strange mother wanting
monuments of womb.

★★★

You need new carpeting
In the foyer, waiting for it
Mandolins stringing
Together a nest
Making soup from
Remember the screech
of blue jays and banjo men
Around the fires of alcoholic
stewing the teeth of deer
slow goat necks and oak trees
Not so different in the burlap
Bags coated in manure
Jingle of vine and seed
From old bear shit
You'd gather after stalking
Ursa Major in heaven

wiping the slime of New England
unloading like a pistol,
    wayfaring stranger and bindles
stewing round burn barrels.
Train cars and rail ties slugged
down with each sip--- the harmonies
    of murderous crows and dust bowls
prairies. Mojo hands rubbing coins
    in cast iron until potent. We cooked
breaking twigs to keep things alive.
Morality saying we can't leave
eyes open after departing
so you drum out each pulse by hand
twice the size of a human heart,
wet in the fields as the wheat weakened
up above the dirt in your boots.

Empty Bottles

The sky is some tribal terror dancing in the shadows
as I carried mountains into nowhere,
forging myself in the burning tires and pallet fires
of old men who've been chasing Jesus on the same plot of farm
for the last sixty years. You can see the dirt in the creases of their hands,
clasped around the green necks as the kids play baseball in the backyards,
every shed window busted from the next great pitcher in the county.
Our dads gave up overtime, teaching us dead-end skills,
how to notch an arrow or string a squirrel snare,
cook the heart of a deer in the last light of November.
Things that matter to nobody now. The old train bridges
give up a little more of themselves to arsonists and alcoholics
who uncoil like severed snakes in the bending light,
as boys get first kisses in their Nana's driveway,
practicing how to feel love on dirt roads.
The gravel kicks up like a copperhead, unsure if it would kill us.

★★★

Cadavers of leggy glass broke fifty
        wide across the fields
        spilling rust on fence posts.

"There's so much sky cluttering here,"
        was all you said about the clouds
        swans (reflecting swans) as you

laid flashing a little bit of blue in the wheat
        the tops dusting you dark,
        heatless and smooth in the

reckless minutes melting with the tar of roadsides.
        A crow in the creases sailing
        eight hundred miles to call

from payphones sneaking a glass and a laugh
        like the bells in a burning church
        as the blimps gloat over

the cut grass of Saturday mornings.
>Out here the juice stains your teeth
>with laughter in places killed animals

are dragged through the wood,
>unraveling in the dark except for bare legs
>on a dirty mattress as the rolling hills get drunk

watching barns stand around, I don't know, forever,
>just laughing at how we still remember the names
>of wild flowers: Tiger Lily, Oxeye, Queen Anne's Lace.

This Rushing

Praying for the endless waving
of earthquakes, cursing into voiceless

sounds from the telephone
as it rings through,

plunking down like the lids of
unthreaded saltshakers

complaining against cloudless
drives on the interstate,

forced to watch the violent finger
painting of puzzled angels,

suddenly seeing how Lazarus
never hurried back.

Why Florida Makes Me Sick, 2003-14
In Memory of J.D.

1.

I can't eat
oranges anymore.
I was young
and it was July,
his mother kissing
with violence
in the heat
as we'd ride
back in the
boonies
to drink
beer on
hot shale,
certain days
unripe as
Polaroids,
our spokes
hot with summer
the way Megan
was coming
out of her blouse, finally.
You'd put a chew
in and spit,
me following forever.

2.

They were
so good
for crushing
in cold glasses.
I find a note
from my mother,
the table
covered in
an old sheet,
white as the powders
she tasted while

I practiced
curveballs
against the shed.
Fucking someone
with my name
for pills
as
each beam
balked from
the pitch.
She scribbled in post-it
of your passing
and to get juice after
work.
I take the hit
like his
mother's face,
as she rationed
the pieces
of his body
in yard sale
sized boxes
for all of our
friends.
His peddle bike given to
Gay Corey, who finally
stopped punching
his hips with
safety pins.
Joey wasn't allowed your
Chessboard
after they found
his hash pipe.
The blue tee
stained with
puke on it
given to me
because Paula
always
knew about
the time
we got high

and chased
field mice
in the garage.

3.

At the wake
some kid
was heroically
eating and
stating
another
"Has gone
to seed"
beneath
the weight of my fork.
His limbs
always come back
in lawns, like dandelions.
The shaggy
uncut pieces
growing
along tomb
stones in
one bar towns
where
even dogs
won't piss.
Weed eaters
will leave
traces of
his teeth
smiling
in trailer
parks
abandoned
as the
orange string
unraveling
from the gear
heads hanging
in the garage.

They'll scatter
him for mulch
in school
yards bright
and soft
as the day
we hoisted
bails over
Doc Watson's
shoulder,
our lips
practicing
on each other
for a girl
whose
brother
drove a car
off an
embankment.
I think
she used to be
Samantha,
her adrenal
breasts
pumping
in the
thick grass
where
we used to
always lay
our peddle
bikes.

4.

I squeeze
the fruit
over the sink
until it burns
my hangnails,
goldfinches
outside as

charming as
the sting
of sunshine.
Even now
I hate their
sweetness,
sitting along
the clothes
lines we'd
plink them from
when summer
soured of candy
and Playboys.
We'd pretend to
hear our names
called by
any other
woman but Mom.
We eventually
discovered porn,
your favorite
rag excavated
from a ditch off
county road 29.

5.

The morning
you came back
I drank
pulp-free orange
juice after brushing
my teeth.
I remembered
it was morning.
July.
What was it like
to feel your body
rupture
alone in the woods?
Did the coyotes
dance before

they ate your face?
Is Jesus as beautiful
as our grandmothers said?

6.

My brother is asleep
on the porch,
being bled
dry by
Punkies.
It has been
eleven years.
The bugs,
some of which
were stuck to
a plastic cup
left out
the night before,
are drunk
on the heat
as I gag
and spit
my eggs
in the sink.

How to Love When You're Away

Start with drinking in the driveway
as lightning bugs feel their way around
each other's light.

Empty the moon in your mason jar, slow sips
that flow through you like a trout creek
then head back across the train tracks that carved their

rust into your bones. Check every oak
for a tree stand and arrowheads.
Put a beer can on one of the branches to make it yours.

Throw all your belongings outside
and listen to the ballgame on the radio.
Raise a Jolly Roger with your American Flag.

Count crows and think of her voice
while percolating coffee on the gas stove.

Untie your boots like hay string, let them snake
across the ground like a highway drive with the radio up
as you sing every shitty country song at the top of your lungs
just to get more mountain air.

Ask god for one more changing of the leaves,
let their colors bleed into you as Ursa Major
stretches across the night.

Stand barefoot and let the mosquitoes eat you,
their heavy bodies like mothers filling the house
with elderberry jam, boiled corn and hot peppers
you'd buy from a roadside stand.

Lick your boots for a taste of the cornfields
you'd throw yourself in for hours.
The dirt will always be there to catch you.

Watch the moths bounce off the porch light,
dying to just be a little closer.

Gratitude
Amanda Oaks

Great love & thanks to Kurt & my boys for their constant love & inspiration & for putting up with me while I penned most of these poems. To my Mom & Dad for their boundless love & support, & for raising me right. To Erica for being you & for always being there, I love you. To Kat, I love you & thank you for knowing how to laugh at the shit life hands us & our loved ones. To my family, friends, past lovers & co-workers, brief encounters & Small Town, PA for helping me stir up the spells for most of these poems. To Robert Lee Brewer + Rachel McKibbens for being prompt gurus & sparking a few of these verses. To my Press Sisters, I love you Witches, endlessly. To John Dorsey for being the best small press brother a girl could ask for. To Tammy Brewer, Jessica Dawson, April Michelle Bratten, Rebecca Schumejda & Jason Neese for being so amazing & supportive through the years. To Zach, thank you for teaming up with me on this & letting me see what our world looks like through your eyes, the beautiful nostalgia you brewed up made my bones & belly ache.

Big thanks to the editors of the following, where earlier versions of these poems originally appeared:

Full of Crow: "Ginger" & "Sudden Death, Pap's Passing"

NightBallet Press: "We're On Our Own Out Here"

Not Your Bitch – Poetry Series: "For the Birds, May All Beings Be Well"

Olentangy Review: "How To Remember," "Ginger," & "How To Swim In The Ocean Of Your Bedsheets"

Poems-for-All: "The Train Ride From You" formally titled, "Vishnu: The Train Ride To You"

Remarkable Doorways Online Literary Magazine: "How To Live in the Present"

Stone Highway Review: "How To Stay Strong"

Tears in the Fence: "Ice Storm"

Voicemail Poems: "You Flood"

Walking Is Still Honest: "How To Appear Dangerous"

Words Dance: "If Our Beginning & End Shared a One Bedroom Apartment" & "There is No Shelter in You Anywhere"

Zygote in My Coffee: "Cause & Effect (Saturday Night Bar Fights)"

Gratitude
Zach Fishel

Much love and many thanks to Bryce and Ana, Sage and Jodi, Janek, Wes, Zane and Cheyenne, and mostly my Dad for always keeping the Pirate's game on and the grill hot. I started this book in memory of Pittsburgh's own, Jack Gilbert, who may be the best poet to ever cross the Roberto Clemente Bridge.

Many thanks to the editors of the following:

Fox Chase Review

Lost in Thought

THEthe Poetry

Bong is Bard

The Merida Review

Red Paint Hill

Midwestern Gothic

Amanda Oaks currently lives & loves in Western PA with her love & life partner, they have two loving sons that have filled theirs lives with laughs & lessons. She likes poems that bloody your mouth just to kiss it clean. Enabler, poet, hoop dancer, lippy feminist, multi-passionate artist & the founding editor of Words Dance Publishing, her works have appeared in numerous online & print publications, including *Stirring*, *Dressing Room Poetry Journal*, *Glamour*, *Elle*, *Parenting* & *Artful Blogging*. Her chapbook, *Hurricane Mouth*, was published by NightBallet Press in 2014. She's an ever-growing, always learning, work-in-progress, just like you. You can find all the stuff at: AmandaOaks.com + Words Dance.com

Zach Fishel was born in Central Pennsylvania and always comes home. He's been a hiking and canoe guide, outdoor educator and university professor. At present he is residing in North Dakota and teaching on a reservation. His poetry has received multiple Pushcart and Best of the Web Nominations. He is the author of *Windsock Etiquette* via Red Paint Hill Press as well as chapbooks from NightBallet Press. He still believes he can be an astronaut, cowboy, and a hobo.

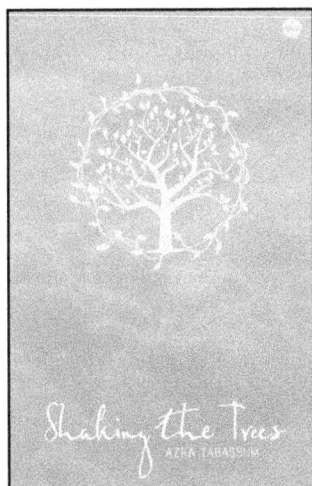

SHAKING THE TREES
Poetry by Azra Tabassum

| $12 | 72 pages | 5.5" x 8.5" | softcover |

ISBN: 978-0692232408

From the very first page *Shaking the Trees* meets you at the edge of the forest, extends a limb & seduces you into taking a walk through the dark & light of connection. Suddenly, like a gunshot in the very-near distance, you find yourself traipsing though a full-blown love story that you can't find your way out of because the story is actually the landscape underneath your feet. It's okay though, you won't get lost– you won't go hungry. Azra shakes every tree along the way so their fruit blankets the ground before you. She picks up pieces & hands them to you but not before she shows you how she can love you so gently it will feel like she's unpeeling you carefully from yourself. She tells you that it isn't about the bite but the warm juice that slips from the lips down chin. She holds your hand when you're trudging through the messier parts, shoes getting stuck in the muck of it all, but you'll keep going with the pulp of the fruit still stuck in-between your teeth, the juice will dry in the crooks of your elbows & in the lines on your palms. You'll taste bittersweet for days.

"I honestly haven't read a collection like this before, or at least I can't remember having read one. My heart was wrecked by Azra. It's like that opening line in Fahrenheit 451 when Bradbury says, "It was a pleasure to burn." It really was a pleasure being wrecked by it."

— **NOURA**
of *NouraReads*

"I wanted to cry and cheer and fuck. I wanted to take the next person I saw and kiss them straight on the lips and say, "Remember this moment for the rest of your life."

— **CHELSEA MILLER**

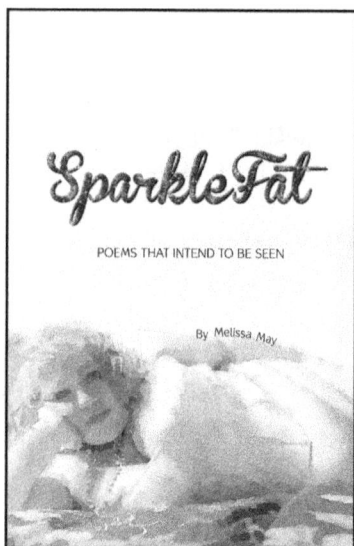

POEMS THAT INTEND TO BE SEEN

By Melissa May

SPARKLEFAT

Poetry by Melissa May

| $12 | 62 pages | 5.5" x 8.5" | softcover |

SparkleFat is a loud, unapologetic, intentional book of poetry about my body, about your body, about fat bodies and how they move through the world in every bit of their flash and spark and burst. Some of the poems are painful, some are raucous celebrations, some are reminders and love letters and quiet gifts back to the vessel that has traveled me so gracefully - some are a hymnal of yes, but all of them sparkle. All of them don't mind if you look – really. They built their own house of intention, and they draped that shit in lime green sequins. All of them intend to be seen. All of them have no more fucks to give about a world that wants them to be quiet.

"I didn't know how much I needed this book until I found myself, three pages in, ugly crying on the plane next to a concerned looking business man. This book is the most glorious, glittery pink permission slip. It made me want to go on a scavenger hunt for every speck of shame in my body and sing hot, sweaty R&B songs to it. There is no voice more authentic, generous and resounding than Melissa May. From her writing, to her performance, to her role in the community she delivers fierce integrity & staggering passion. From the first time I watched her nervously step to the mic, to the last time she crushed me in a slam, it is has been an honor to watch her astound the poetry slam world and inspire us all to be not just better writers but better people. We need her.

— LAUREN ZUNIGA
Author of *The Smell of Good Mud*

"*SparkleFat* is a firework display of un-shame. Melissa May's work celebrates all of the things we have been so long told deserved no streamers. This collection invites every fat body out to the dance and steams up the windows in the backseat of the car afterwards by kissing the spots we thought (or even hoped) no one noticed but are deserving of love just the same as our mouths."

— RACHEL WILEY
Author of the forthcoming *Fat Girl Finishing School*

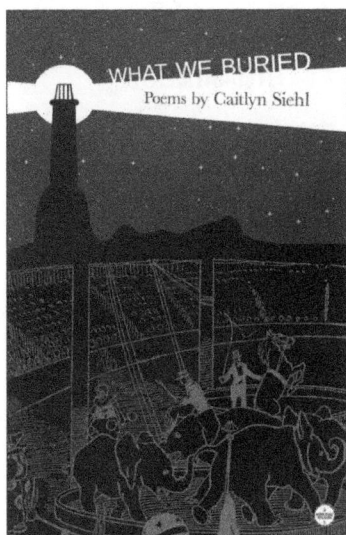

WHAT WE BURIED
Poetry by Caitlyn Siehl

| $12 | 64 pages | 5.5" x 8.5" | softcover |

ISBN: 978-0615985862

This book is a cemetery of truths buried alive. The light draws you in where you will find Caitlyn there digging. When you get close enough, she'll lean in & whisper, Baby, buried things will surface no matter what, get to them before they get to you first. Her unbounded love will propel you to pick up a shovel & help— even though the only thing you want to do is kiss her lips, kiss her hands, kiss every one of her stretch marks & the fire that is raging in pit of her stomach. She'll see your eyes made of devour & sadness, she'll hug you & say, Baby, if you eat me alive, I will cut my way out of your stomach. Don't let this be your funeral. Teach yourself to navigate the wound.

"It takes a true poet to write of love and desire in a way that manages to surprise and excite. Caitlyn Siehl does this in poem after poem and makes it seem effortless. Her work shines with a richness of language and basks in images that continue to delight and astound with multiple readings. What We Buried is a treasure from cover to cover."

— **WILLIAM TAYLOR JR.**
Author of *An Age of Monsters*

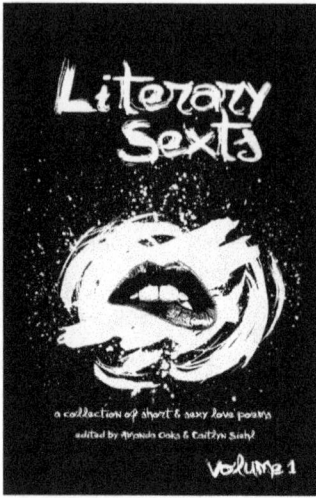

LITERARY SEXTS

A Collection of Short & Sexy Love Poems
(Volume 1)

| $12 | 42 pages | 5.5" x 8.5" | softcover |

ISBN: 978-0615959726

Literary Sexts is a modern day anthology of short love poems with subtle erotic undertones edited by Amanda Oaks & Caitlyn Siehl. Hovering around 50 contributors & 124 poems, this book reads is like one long & very intense conversation between two lovers. It's absolutely breathtaking. These are poems that you would text to your lover. Poems that you would slip into a back pocket, suitcase, wallet or purse on the sly. Poems that you would write on slips of paper & stick under your crush's windshield wiper. Poems that you would write on a Post-it note & leave on the bathroom mirror.

**HIT #1
ON AMAZON'S
HOT NEW
RELEASE LIST!**

"It's like 100+ new ways to make a reader blush. The imagery is so subtle yet completely thrilling..."
NOW I NEED A COLD SHOWER!"
                                                    - K. W.

"**I DEVOURED IT!** I physically wanted to eat these poems. I wanted to wear them on my skin like perfume..."
                                                    - A. G.

"I have consumed this in ways that have left my insides looking like strips of velvet fabric... **SO ORGASMIC!**"
                                                    - K. B.

"**A MAELSTROM OF EMOTIONS!** I only hope that there is a Volume 2, a Volume 3 and so on because I need more of this!"
                                                    - Daniel CZ

Other titles available from
WORDS DANCE PUBLISHING

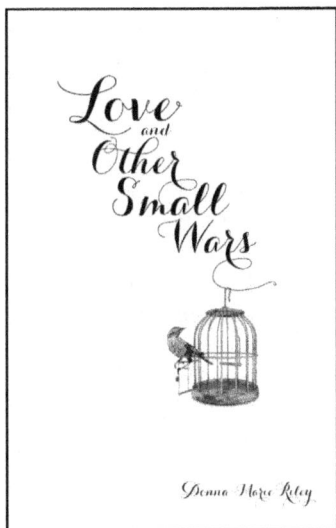

LOVE AND OTHER SMALL WARS

Poetry by Donna-Marie Riley

| $12 | 76 pages | 5.5" x 8.5" | softcover |

ISBN: 978-0615931111

Love and Other Small Wars reminds us that when you come back from combat usually the most fatal of wounds are not visible. Riley's debut collection is an arsenal of deeply personal poems that embody an intensity that is truly impressive yet their hands are tender. She enlists you. She gives you camouflage & a pair of boots so you can stay the course through the minefield of her heart. You will track the lovely flow of her soft yet fierce voice through a jungle of powerful imagery on womanhood, relationships, family, grief, sexuality & love, amidst other matters. Battles with the heart aren't easily won but Riley hits every mark. You'll be relieved that you're on the same side. Much like war, you'll come back from this book changed.

"Riley's work is wise, intense, affecting, and uniquely crafted. This collection illuminates her ability to write with both a gentle hand and a bold spirit. She inspires her readers and creates an indelible need inside of them to consume more of her exceptional poetry. I could read *Love and Other Small Wars* all day long…and I did."

— **APRIL MICHELLE BRATTEN**
editor of *Up the Staircase Quarterly*

"Riley's poems are personal, lyrical and so vibrant they practically leap off the page, which also makes them terrifying at times. A beautiful debut."

— **BIANCA STEWART**

Other titles available from
WORDS DANCE PUBLISHING

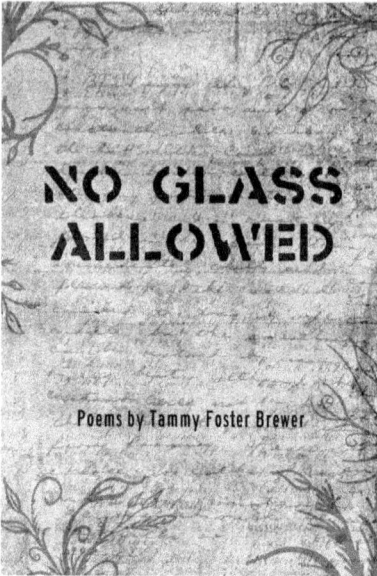

Tammy Foster Brewer is the type of poet who makes me wish I could write poetry instead of novels. From motherhood to love to work, Tammy's poems highlight the extraordinary in the ordinary and leave the reader wondering how he did not notice what was underneath all along. I first heard Tammy read 'The Problem is with Semantics' months ago, and it's stayed with me ever since. Now that I've read the entire collection, I only hope I can make room to keep every one of her poems in my heart and mind tomorrow and beyond.

— **NICOLE ROSS**, author

NO GLASS ALLOWED
Poetry by Tammy Foster Brewer

$12 | 56 pages | 6" x 9" | softcover | ISBN: 978-0615870007

Brewer's collection is filled with uncanny details that readers will wear like the accessories of womanhood. Fishing the Chattahoochee, sideways trees, pollen on a car, white dresses and breast milk, and so much more -- all parts of a deeply intellectual pondering of what is often painful and human regarding the other halves of mothers and daughters, husbands and wives, lovers and lost lovers, children and parents.

— **NICHOLAS BELARDES**
author of *Songs of the Glue Machines*

Tammy deftly juxtaposes distinct imagery with stories that seem to collide in her brilliant poetic mind. Stories of transmissions and trees and the words we utter, or don't. Of floods and forgiveness, conversations and car lanes, bread and beginnings, awe and expectations, desire and leaps of faith that leave one breathless, and renewed.

"When I say I am a poet / I mean my house has many windows" has to be one of the best descriptions of what it's like to be a contemporary female poet who not only holds down a day job and raises a family, but whose mind and heart regularly file away fleeting images and ideas that might later be woven into something permanent, and perhaps even beautiful. This ability is not easily acquired. It takes effort, and time, and the type of determination only some writers, like Tammy, possess and are willing to actively exercise.

— **KAREN DEGROOT CARTER**
author of *One Sister's Song*

WHAT TO
DO AFTER
SHE SAYS
NO

a poem by kris ryan

Unrequited love? We've all been there.

Enter:

WHAT TO DO AFTER SHE SAYS NO
by Kris Ryan.

This skillfully designed 10-part poem explores what it's like to ache for someone. This is the book you buy yourself or a friend when you are going through a breakup or a one-sided crush, it's the perfect balance between aha, humor & heartbreak.

WHAT TO DO AFTER SHE SAYS NO
A Poem by Kris Ryan

$10 | 104 pages | 5" x 8" | softcover | ISBN: 978-0615870045

"*What to Do After She Says No* takes us from Shanghai to the interior of a refrigerator, but mostly dwells inside the injured human heart, exploring the aftermath of emotional betrayal. This poem is a compact blast of brutality, with such instructions as "Climb onto the roof and jump off. If you break your leg, you are awake. If you land without injury, pinch and twist at your arm until you wake up." Ryan's use of the imperative often leads us to a reality where pain is the only outcome, but this piece is not without tenderness, and certainly not without play, with sounds and images ricocheting off each other throughout. Anticipate the poetry you wish you knew about during your last bad breakup; this poem offers a first "foothold to climb out" from that universal experience."

— **LISA MANGINI**

"Reading Kris Ryan's *What To Do After She Says No* is like watching your heart pound outside of your chest. Both an unsettling visual experience and a hurricane of sadness and rebirth—this book demands more than just your attention, it takes a little bit of your soul, and in the end, makes everything feel whole again."

— **JOHN DORSEY**
author of ***Tombstone Factory***

"*What to Do After She Says No* is exquisite. Truly, perfectly exquisite. It pulls you in on a familiar and wild ride of a heart blown open and a mind twisting in an effort to figure it all out. It's raw and vibrant...and in the same breath comforting. I want to crawl inside this book and live in a world where heartache is expressed so magnificently.

— **JO ANNA ROTHMAN**
MA, Coach & Conjurer of Electric Creative Wholeness

WORDS DANCE PUBLISHING has one aim:

To spread mind-blowing / heart-opening poetry.

Words Dance artfully & carefully wrangles words that were born to dance wildly in the heart-mind matrix. Rich, edgy, raw, emotionally-charged energy balled up & waiting to whip your eyes wild; we rally together words that were written to make your heart go boom right before they slay your mind. We like Poems that sneak up on you. Poems that make out with you. Poems that bloody your mouth just to kiss it clean. Poems that bite your cheek so you spend all day tonguing the wound. Poems that vandalize your heart. Poems that act like a tin can phone connecting you to your childhood. Fire Alarm Poems. Glitterbomb Poems. Jailbreak Poems. Poems that could marry the land or the sea; that are both the hero & the villain. Poems that are the matches when there is a city-wide power outage. Poems that throw you overboard just dive in & save your ass. Poems that push you down on the stoop in front of history's door screaming at you to knock. Poems that are soft enough to fall asleep on. Poems that will still be clinging to the walls inside of your bones on your 90th birthday. We like poems. Submit yours.

Words Dance Publishing is an independent press out of Pennsylvania. We work closely & collaboratively with all of our writers to ensure that their words continue to breathe in a sound & stunning home. Most importantly though, we leave the windows in these homes unlocked so you, the reader, can crawl in & throw one fuck of a house party.

To learn more about our books, authors, events & Words Dance Poetry Magazine, visit:

WORDSDANCE.COM